The Collected Hymns

of John Haynes Holmes

The Collected Hymns

of John Haynes Holmes

Beacon Press   Beacon Hill   Boston

Dedication

To Madeleine, Roger, and Frances, my well-beloved.

Acknowledgments

To Henry Wilder Foote, who suggested this book and
cooperated in its preparation.

To Edward Darling, of the Beacon Press, and his staff,
who, with unquenchable enthusiasm looked to the
publication of the book.

To Flora Schneider and Alice Smith, my secretaries, who,
with zeal and utter devotion, put my manuscript in
shape and made it one of the "handsomest" ever seen
by the printer.

To "Don" Harrington, whose cooperation was unfailing.

To my congregation, who have stood by their minister
through more than fifty years of vicissitude and peril.

Statements

This is my last book. As such it is my farewell to friends, known and unknown to me, whose interest and sympathy, especially in these last years, have helped me immeasurably to carry on and finish my work. To see one's work unfinished, or perhaps never to be finished, is sadness unutterable. But this sadness I have been spared. Therefore am I able to leave this book as my heritage to those I love.

Table of Contents

Book III

Index of First Lines

Introduction: Hymns and Hymnists

O come, let us sing unto the Lord . . .
Let us come before his presence with
thanksgiving, and make a joyful
noise unto him with psalms.

BOOK OF PSALMS

I was quoted once as saying that I would rather write one hymn that would sing its way into the human heart and there be remembered than preach a hundred eloquent sermons.

I do not remember making this statement, but I may have made it. It fits me. I have always been interested in hymns as a native and noble expression of the soul. I have believed that the hymn today, like the psalm yesterday, has been the purest expression of the religious sentiment. I have been ambitious, in a mild sort of way, to write a hymn of my own that might travel far and endure long. Through all my life I have tried my hand at writing hymns. While some of these have appeared to me not unimportant, the majority have seemed commonplace and the general level mediocre, with the result that I have been indifferent and careless in handling these products of my heart and pen. I have kept no portfolio or filing cabinet, but have left them to be mislaid, forgotten, or lost. Now has come this un-expected opportunity to publish my collected hymns in permanent and handsome form. "Collected"! Alas, it would be more accurate to speak of them as "scattered." But such as are known to me, or are to be found, have been gathered together in this volume for such use as may be made of it.

I

Statistics often have considerable public importance and not infrequently personal interest as well. May I therefore set down the number of hymns gathered together in this place, their dates (if available), their usage and present rating (if that may be judged)? In a period of a half century, I find I have written forty or more hymns— a modest total as compared with the prolific utterance of Charles Wesley, for example, who wrote some 6,500; but a not unimpressive number in its own right. Many of these hymns have disappeared with the occasions that produced them, but eight have been salvaged and published in *Hymns of the Spirit*,[1] the best, and one of the most widely read, hymnals of our time.

Dr. Tweedy, in his remarkable hymn collection, *Christian Worship and Praise*,[2] has rescued seven of my compositions; and these are likely to last, as Dr. Tweedy's book shows abundant signs of permanency. Especially gratifying is the placing of five of my hymns in the *Union Hymnal for Jewish Worship*.[3] Astonishing it is to discover in the *Army and Navy Hymnal*[4] two of my lesser-known hymns. Pretty good for a red-hot pacifist! On the National Day of Prayer set aside in 1914 for prayers for peace in all the churches and synagogues of the land, my now familiar hymn "God of the Nations, Near and Far" was appointed and sung as the official hymn of the occasion. At the General Conference of the Unitarians, held in Montreal, Canada, in September, 1917, my hymn "O'er Continent and Ocean" was sung as dedicated to this gathering. This gave me a special satisfaction, as it was the hymn I have come to regard as the best international and interracial hymn I have written. This had added significance in the fact that I was serving that year as Chairman of the Conference.

The more general use of my hymns among the various denominations of Christendom is perhaps worth noting. I have found in nearly all more recent hymnals from one to three or five of my hymns, variously chosen and thus showing differences in taste and expression in this important field of religious sentiment. I have in my library two crowded shelves of hymnals, representing nearly all of the

[1] Boston: Beacon Press, 1938.
[2] Tweedy, Henry Hallam (ed.). New York: Harper, 1939.
[3] Compiled by Central Conference of American Rabbis. 1932.
[4] Bennett, Ivan L. (ed.). New York: A. S. Barnes & Co., 1941.

great groups among the Protestant churches of this country, and there are probably others unknown to me. The total number of these hymnals is seventy-five or more, and includes such denominations as the Universalist, Congregational, Methodist, Presbyterian, Baptist, the Brethren, the Friends, the Anglican Church of England, and various independent hymnals, such as the well-known *Social Hymns* and Dr. Tweedy's volume already cited.

The foreign adventures of my hymns are a story in themselves. It is now not an altogether unusual experience to find "The Voice of God is Calling" in an English hymn book. During the war, reports came to me of my hymns being sung in army camps on both sides of the line—the influence, probably, of some liberal-minded chaplains who had strayed unexpectedly into the Army and Navy. But nothing can compare with the excitement I felt when I received some years ago a Japanese hymnal containing three of my hymns. Incidentally, I may say that a hymnist who has not seen his compositions printed in the Japanese script has something still to live for.

II

It was after I had written a hymn or two in my early ministry, and was enjoying a certain pride in the achievement, that I first heard the now embarrassingly familiar saying, "It takes a third-rate poet to write a first-rate hymn." At first I was prone to attribute this saying to the jealousy of one who could not write even a fourth-rate hymn. But, on studying the matter, I found that there is a real distinction here that calls for some kind of explanation.

There is no question but that a considerable number of well-known English and American poets of high rank appear in our hymnals. Thus, in one of the best of the contemporary volumes, I find such names as Joseph Addison, William Blake, Robert Bridges, William Cullen Bryant, Gilbert K. Chesterton, Arthur Hugh Clough,

5

William Cowper, John Dryden, Ralph Waldo Emerson, George Herbert, Oliver Wendell Holmes, Rudyard Kipling, Henry Wadsworth Longfellow, James Russell Lowell, Edwin Markham, John Milton, Thomas Moore, Christina Rossetti, Walter Scott, Edward Rowland Sill, John Addington Symonds, Alfred Tennyson, William Watson, and John Greenleaf Whittier. This seems to be a not unimpressive list, containing the names of at least two poets of front-rank fame—Dryden and Milton. But it is doubtful if many of these poets can be described as hymn-writers in the true sense of the word. The hymns associated with their names are most of them adaptations, or else poems written quite apart from any thought of their use in churches for purposes of religious worship, while others would seem to be happy accidents, such as Kipling's "Recessional" and Emerson's "We Love the Venerable House." A few—Symonds' "These Things Shall Be," for example!—are not hymns at all. Of all these poets I would describe only Bryant, Cowper, O. W. Holmes, and Whittier as genuine hymnists. And no one of these is a poet of the first or even second order.

On the other hand, who are the great writers of hymns? I would list without hesitation such names as Horatius Bonar, Sir John Bowring, Stopford Brooke, John White Chadwick, Philip Doddridge, John Ellerton, Frederick William Faber, Washington Gladden, William Channing Gannett, Thomas Hornblower Gill, Frances Ridley Havergal, Henry Warburton Hawkes, Reginald Heber, Frederick Lucian Hosmer, Samuel Johnson, Marion Franklin Ham, Samuel Longfellow, George Matheson, James Montgomery, Eliza Scudder, Edmund Hamilton Sears, William George Tarrant, Isaac Watts, Charles Wesley, and Theodore C. Williams. Other names come to mind, such as Sarah Flower Adams ("Nearer, My God, to Thee"), Henry Francis Lyte ("Abide with Me"), Phillips Brooks ("O Little Town of Bethlehem"), and John Henry Newman ("Lead, Kindly Light").

Of all these, which one has any primary rating as a

poet? In anthologies of English poetry here on my desk, I note the inclusion only of Isaac Watts. The others, so far as poetry is concerned, do not exist at all.

The contrast between poets as hymn-writers and hymn-writers as poets is dramatized in the case of the brothers Longfellow. Henry Wadsworth Longfellow was a poet of very considerable proportions, as we are beginning to learn now in these days. His name appears in some hymnals, but only as the author of "I Heard the Bells on Christmas Day," which was never intended as a hymn and is poorly adapted to this purpose. His one genuine hymn, written for his brother Samuel's ordination into the ministry, was excellent in sentiment but a failure in composition. Samuel Longfellow, on the other hand, wrote many hymns—no less than twenty-seven in the latest hymnal I have consulted. Some of these are adaptations, but the rest are original and among the noblest in our language. Yet Samuel Longfellow has no place at all as a poet. His famous brother does not so much obscure him as shine alone in the literary firmament.

III

It would seem, from this little analysis, that there is perhaps some truth in the unkind suggestion that only poor poets make good hymn-writers. The great poets, at any rate, do not flourish in the field of hymnology, and the great hymn-writers almost never win distinction as poets. What is the explanation of this dichotomy between poets and hymnists?

The answer, I believe, is to be found in the fact that hymnology represents a distinct form of literary art, having about the same relation to poetry that prayer has to prose. It is a type of composition that exists of and by itself, and thus possesses qualities that are uniquely and nobly its own.

A hymn must be simple. It must contain not the

7

slightest suggestion of complexity, either of thought or of expression. There must be no unusual words, no fanciful figures of speech, no elaboration of diction or phrase. Those very devices of eloquence and beauty which the poet commands, as the composer commands the instruments in his orchestra, are here quite out of place. Simplicity is the word—simplicity, which is the handmaid of clarity.

Secondly, a hymn must be characterized by feeling rather than by thought. It must appeal primarily to the heart, and not to the mind. Of course, it must have a central idea or theme, but this theme must not be so much developed by an intellectual process as quickened by a spiritual emotion. It must be stated, not argued and amplified, and then suffused with the glow and radiance of exalted sentiment. A good hymn must stir and lift the soul; must comfort, challenge, and inspire.

Lastly, a hymn must draw its idea or theme from the familiar materials of life. Its range may extend from the sublime regions of the heavens to the intimate recesses of the heart. It may chant the vast concepts of time and eternity, as in Isaac Watts's "O God, Our Help in Ages Past," or catalogue the simple sentiments of personal dedication, as in Frances Havergal's "Take My Life and Let It Be," which, we are told, was one of Gandhi's favorite Christian hymns. It may deal with great traditions of faith and hope and love, or mark transitions to new stages of spiritual apprehension, as in the social hymnology of our day. But always it must dwell where the heart of man is more or less at home. A hymn is a prayer; it is the soul lifting itself from its daily lot to communion with the Most High. Therefore it must begin with what it knows, and only then reach out to what it dares to dream.

The noblest hymns are those which have sprung from the inner genius of a people—the Psalms on the one hand, the Negro spirituals on the other! At the nethermost extremity of these supernal achievements lies the great mass of Christian, or rather Protestant, hymns—hymns that are all too often doggerel of the worst description. After the

8

august medieval hymnology, how great was the fall into the sheer vulgarity of these revivalistic songs. The average Protestant hymnbook of the last century, while yet acknowledging and using some of the best hymns, is none the less an almost hopeless omnium-gatherum of literary and spiritual trash, illustrating how easy is the descent from the simple and natural to the obviously cheap and sentimental.

It is here that the hymn-writer dowered with any genuine gift must do his work. This work is to take these simple emotions of the heart, emotions that emerge from experiences of daily living interpreted as a quest for God, and express them in terms of simplicity, dignity, and exaltation of spirit. He must not write a poem—the hymn is no competitor of the epic, or the lyric, or the ode, or the elegy! It lies quite outside the scope of the poet, as wood-carving lies outside the scope of the sculptor, and etching of the painter. The hymn is *sui generis*—the product of an art that has its own qualities, to be achieved only by a submission to a technique as difficult as it is distinctive. The poet may master this technique, but usually he does not. He either is not interested in hymns, or is inhibited by the very qualities of true poesy that make him what he is. There is, however, a modest order of spiritual craftsmen who, like Browning's Abt Vogler, "understand." And to them is given the divine privilege of singing the soul's songs to God.

IV

An illustration is more convincing than all the exposition in the world. Let me therefore point a moral and adorn my tale by citing two hymns, one of which is bad and the other superlatively good.

The first is my own hymn "When darkness, brooding o'er the deep." This is a noble poem—indeed, as an expression in poetic form showing the progress of mankind through the ages gone, it is, within its own limitations, a poem superbly done. But as a hymn, it has most serious faults. It is primarily intellectual in character: it presents an idea, and only incidentally an emotion. Furthermore, the line of thought is not simple, but difficult, hardly to be appreciated by worshipers not conversant with nineteenth-century science and philosophy. At bottom the hymn deals with abstractions, and thus is understandable only by those well trained in objective thought. It just happens that the work has application to tragic events of our time, but not as a hymn, either in form or in circumstance. This is the reason, I have no doubt, that the hymn made not the slightest impression when it was published, and has, to all intents and purposes, long since disappeared.

In contrast to this is William Pierson Merrill's superb hymn:

> Rise up, O men of God!
> Have done with lesser things,
> Give heart and soul and mind and strength
> To serve the King of kings.

It would be difficult to praise this hymn too highly. As a poem, it is valueless. But as a hymn, it has everything a hymn should have. It is brief, simple, clear, picturesque, challenging—a perfect example of the commonplace lifted to the sublime. No congregation ever sang this hymn without being inspired. Dr. Merrill was himself inspired when he wrote it. Match my potent poetizing with Dr. Merrill's glad shout of faith, and you realize at once what is good and not so good in a hymn.

It is not difficult, from this point of view, to discover the great hymns. A few that occur to me, apart from those already named, are Luther's "A Mighty Fortress Is Our God"; Sill's "Send Down Thy Truth, O God"; O. W. Holmes's "Lord of All Being, Throned Afar"; Collyer's "Unto Thy Temple, Lord, We Come"; Gladden's "O Master, Let Me Walk With Thee"; Chesterton's "O God of Earth and Altar"; Matheson's "O Love That Wilt Not Let Me Go"; Longfellow's "O Life That Maketh All Things

New"; Hosmer's "Thy Kingdom Come, O God"; and Johnson's "Life of Ages, Richly Poured." The greatest lines ever written in any hymn are Frederick W. Faber's:

> There's a wideness in God's mercy,
> Like the wideness of the sea. . . .

Had Faber been able to keep up to the level of these majestic lines, he would have produced in this case the greatest of all hymns.

Of the hymns just named, only Oliver Wendell Holmes's and Chesterton's can be regarded as having any claims to being poetry—and they are not better but perhaps worse hymns on that account. The others are fashioned of a different texture. They are noble specimens of a different and wholly distinctive art form. They stand or fall not as poems at all but as *hymns*—that is, on their own inherent merits. It is time, high time, that hymnology be recognized and reverenced for itself alone, and thus rescued at last from its lowly station as a kind of poor relation of poetry, and lifted to its proper place as the soul in tune with God.

v

I was looking over the so-called Olney Hymns of William Cowper the other day, and was impressed by the skill of this poet in opening his hymns with lines of mystic beauty or high-sounding proclamation. It is no secret that Cowper was a master of the noble phrase. Witness such lines as those in Book II of *The Task,* where he speaks of certain men of his time in England who

> Presume to lay their hand upon the ark
> Of her magnificent and awful cause.

This same poem includes the famous passage in which Cowper denounces slavery and extols the tradition of English liberty:

> Slaves cannot breathe in England; if their lungs
> Receive our air, that moment they are free;
> They touch our country, and their shackles fall.

And who can forget the lines in which he yearns for "a lodge in some vast wilderness"

> Where rumor of oppression and deceit,
> Of unsuccessful or successful war
> Might never reach me more.

Cowper is neglected, not merely because of his eighteenth-century manners and ideas, but more because he lacked both the physical and spiritual vitality to maintain the highest levels of poetic utterance. Had he not been "a stricken deer," as he called himself, he might have matched Miltonic splendors.

It is this power of occasional eloquence, of the noble and sonorous phrase, which Cowper used with such effectiveness in his hymns, especially in the opening lines. He got his hymns off to a good start, which I deem to be as important an element in hymn-writing as in boat-racing. Note such first lines as these:

> Oh! for a closer walk with God,
> A calm and heavenly frame. . . .

> Hark! my soul, it is the Lord!

> God moves in a mysterious way
> His wonders to perform. . . .

> Sometimes a light surprises
> The Christian while he sings. . . .

> The billows swell, the winds are high. . . .

These lines sound a call; they catch a vision; they distill an atmosphere. They insure the success of the hymn in the first dozen words. Can any hymn be successful that does not thus begin?

An examination of the "Index of First Lines" in any contemporary hymnal will show how superb are the opening lines of most of our widely accepted hymns. Perhaps the truth is that the hymns that have survived the rigorous test of usage are those whose opening phrases are worthy to be listed in an "Index of First Lines"! But commonplace first lines are plentiful. In a book that I have here before me as I write, a book widely used in our more liberal churches, I find lines that are dull and colorless, indicating little or nothing of the thought and spirit of a hymn—phrases that anyone might have written, routine apostrophes or exclamations that kindle no light and stir no feeling. These lines never get off the ground, so to speak. One wonders that hymns thus introduced could have had vitality enough to have endured at all.

Try it for yourself, and see if it is not true that commonplace first lines are the tags of commonplace hymns, which, like commonplace men, are necessarily in the majority. Such hymns, like such men, have their place and use, I have no doubt; but they carry with them little inspiration.

But in this hymnal at my hand there are also great first lines, which are the open doors to great hymns. Or, to put it the other way 'round, great hymns almost invariably have noble entrances. Read down through the index, and see how these first lines run:

A mighty fortress is our God. . . .

Could the man who conceived that line have written anything other than an immortal hymn?

Abide with me, fast falls the eventide.

How different from the one before, yet how true to song and sense! The whole of life and death unfolds from those seven words.

Awake, my soul, stretch every nerve. . . .

A trumpet call that sounds clear to the very end of this great hymn!
And many more:

Faith of our fathers, living still. . . .

Go forth to life, O child of earth!

13

God's trumpet wakes the slumbering world. . . .

I saw the City of the Lord. . . .

In the cross of Christ I glory. . . .

Lord of all being, throned afar. . . .

O Master, let me walk with thee. . . .

Rise, God, judge thou the earth in might. . . .

Rise up, O men of God!

The spacious firmament on high. . . .

Watchman, tell us of the night. . . .

When wilt thou save the people?

These are but a few that catch my eye. Others may choose as many more. The truth remains: all that a hymn would say must sound, or at least be suggested, in its opening line. Failing that line, it is doubtful if the hymn can ever live, and burn, and guide the hearts of men.

VI

The closing lines of a hymn are also important, though not so easy to trace or to define. They should certainly contain the spiritual summary of all that the hymn has been trying to say. They should have something of the surety and calm and power of a great ship moving into port after an ocean voyage. Compact in their few words must be the essence of the hymn's flight through four, five, or six verses, as in the ship there lies the cargo borne across as many seas. As the first lines give the announcement, or proclamation, of the hymn, so the last lines must speak the benediction. At the start, excitement; at the close, satisfaction and sweet content.

One way of solving the problem of the close of a hymn is to write the piece around a refrain, repeated in verse after verse, with or without variation. The classic example of this method in our time is Kipling's use of the famous couplet that concludes each stanza of "Recessional":

> Lord God of hosts, be with us yet,
> Lest we forget, lest we forget!

Another familiar example is Faber's "Faith of Our Fathers," each verse of which ends with the rousing pledge:

> Faith of our fathers, holy faith,
> We will be true to thee till death.

A simple and effective device is that of repeating at the close of a hymn the line, or lines, that opened it. This echo, as it may be called, is like ending the movement of a symphony with a final proclamation of the opening theme. Isaac Watts does this superbly in his famous hymn "O God, Our Help in Ages Past," where the first verse, with the change of a single line, is used also as the last verse, as follows:

> O God, our help in ages past,
> Our hope for years to come,
> Be thou our guard while troubles last,
> And our eternal home.

In the old days, when Christian theology was prone to regard this present life as only a preparation for the life to come beyond the grave, it was easy to end a hymn as Watts does—with a reference to heaven. Sometimes this was the logic of the theme, more often not; but it was frequently used, and still is. Run through any hymnal and see how many hymns end with some such lines as these:

> I taste e'en now the hallowed bliss
> Of an eternal home.
>
> To sing the songs of victory
> With faithful souls above.
>
> Forward tends to his abode
> To rest in his embrace.
>
> Lead me to my journey's end.

Cardinal Newman glorified this custom in the closing lines of his "Lead, Kindly Light":

> And with the morn those angel faces smile
> Which I have loved long since, and lost awhile.

The noblest way of ending a hymn is to lead its ideas along to a mounting climax of thought and feeling which breaks out in the last verse as a kind of inevitable chorale, the statement and celebration of all that the hymn is about. Oliver Wendell Holmes does this in his magnificent "Lord of All Being," the last verse of which reads:

> Grant us thy truth to make us free,
> And kindling hearts that burn for thee,
> Till all thy living altars claim
> One holy light, one heavenly flame.

Frederick Lucian Hosmer ends his "Thy Kingdom Come, O Lord" with the unforgettable:

> Till rise at last, to span
> Its firm foundations broad,
> The commonwealth of man,
> The city of our God.

And what can match the perfection of the last lines of Theodore C. Williams' hymn of brotherhood:

> When thy heart enfolds a brother,
> God is there.

Some closing lines are unbelievably weak. See "We Go Not on a Pilgrimage" by Jones Very, who was a true poet:

> We go not on a pilgrimage
> As those who went of old;
> The Holy Land around us lies,
> *Of which we have been told.*

Others are like "a grand amen" in a cathedral. See the close of Montgomery's hymn on prayer:

> Lord, teach us how to pray.

A hymn may be made or lost with its closing as with its opening lines.

All of this may seem trivial. Yet it is of intense interest to those of us who love hymns. And it should be of importance to those who must deal with hymnology—ministers, for example, who lead their people to the rich pastures, or to the sterile wastes, of our church hymnals!

What I would convey is the idea that hymns represent an art, a literary and spiritual art, as real as music, painting, or poesy. It is a rare art, as delicate as the carving of ivory or the molding of chased gold. It is a difficult art, mastered by only a few through many ages, but infinitely rewarding.

VII

Nothing of all that I have done, or tried to do, gives me on the whole such satisfaction as my writing of hymns. This represents a small segment of achievement, as compared with the two thousand and more sermons I have prepared and preached and published in the active period of my ministry. It measures up to no such personal level of excellence as that attained and held by outstanding expounders of the Word. As a sheer expenditure of energy aimed at high purposes, the pulpit still stands unrivaled. But the hymn has a quality of its own, rare and beautiful, which makes the composition of these sacred songs a spiritual event. I rejoice that among my hymns are a few that have won favor and use. My chief abounding satisfaction on this score attaches itself to my hymn "The Voice of God is Calling."

In September, 1913, I was returning on the S.S. *Laconia* to America, after a summer of delightful travel in England, Scotland, and Wales. Before leaving on this trip, I had promised a committee of the Young People's Religious Union (Unitarian), in charge of a convention in the fall, to write a special hymn adapted and dedicated to the

17

occasion; and here I was on a swift ship headed for New York, and not a line of my hymn written. I had tried my hand at composition several times without result, except failure. Then, suddenly, there came within me a veritable explosion of energy. In a few hours I had before me on paper just what I wanted, my promised hymn to be. In a few days I was listening to my words sung by a chorus of voices, fresh and lifted up. How does one explain such things? Do they just happen, or is this a genuine instance of the spirit? Who can tell?

A final cause for satisfaction is that at least two of my hymns seem to be headed for immortality. "The Voice of God is Calling" shows every sign of survival. The same is true, and far less worthily, I think, of my hymn "O Father, Thou Who Givest All." These two, and perhaps in the long run one or two others still awaiting recognition, will pass from generation to generation, a living influence of light.

Then will come the crowning glory of this immortality of which I speak. On some day in the near or distant future, two persons will be at church singing with the congregation a hymn.

"See," whispers one to the other, "this hymn was written by John Haynes Holmes," and points at the name printed at the upper left-hand corner of the tune.

"John Haynes Holmes," repeats the other in evident perplexity. "Holmes? Holmes! Is that the famous judge? I didn't know he wrote hymns."

Book I

Processional Hymn

Tune—"Antioch" (Georg Friedrich Handel)

Note: A hymn of reunion, written in 1920, which first appeared in *Hymns of the Spirit*. It was set deliberately to the difficult but magnificent tune of "Antioch" as an experiment in versification.

Joy to our hearts! Again we meet!
    Let prayer and praise abound!
As rivers to the ocean's tide,
As iron to the magnet's side,
    We come with hasting feet,
    Our comrades all to greet,
    And holy vows repeat,
        With gladsome sound.

Rise, comrades true, in strength and love!
    The Lord awaiteth ye!
He speaketh in your faithful word;
He fighteth with your valiant sword.
    His trust and patience prove,
    In high allegiance move,
    Till earth, like heaven above,
        Is glad and free.

Shout and rejoice, ye people all!
    The days of hate shall cease!
Let justice and good will be done,
Let fellowship be surely won,
    And round this whirling ball
    The tribes of men shall call,
    And stand like angels tall,
        In love and peace.

The Day of Wrath

Tune—"Melita" (John Bacchus Dykes)

Note: Unpublished, unused, unknown—this hymn, written in 1918, was a product of the times. It exposed the agony, horrors, and sin of mankind's resort to arms.

O thou, who in chaotic night
Turned darkness into flaming light;
Whose spirit moved upon the sea,
And raised the hills in majesty:
We turn to thee in sin and shame,
And call again thy sacred name.

Behold the labor of our years
Transformed to ashes, blood, and tears;
The temples of our boasted trust
Cast down in wreckage to the dust;
Each tow'ring pillar overthrown,
Each lifted idol scarred and prone.

The Day of Wrath, that dreadful day
Hath doomed us on our evil way;
Found out our trust in Mammon's breed,
Our sowing of the iron seed,
Our love of sceptres and the sword,
Our flouting of thy sacred word.

But thou, O God, canst save us still;
Steadfast abides thy holy will.
Again, from out the pit of night,
Will break the miracle of light.
Forgive us, Lord, our sins confess'd;
Bring in the Kingdom of the Bless'd.

Prayer for Peace

Tune—"St. Agnes" (John Bacchus Dykes)

Note: Written and first published in the *Unitarian Hymn and Tune Book* (1914). The Great War had just broken out in Europe, and the movement to keep us out of it—under the slogan "No More War"—commanded public attention.

The churches of the country proclaimed in this crisis a Peace Sunday for special services of intercession in which Catholics, Protestants, and Jews might join their voices on behalf of peace. At these services, attended by great throngs of people throughout the nation, this hymn was appointed to be sung.

God of the nations, near and far,
    Ruler of all mankind,
Bless thou thy peoples as they strive
    The paths of peace to find.

The clash of arms still shakes the sky,
    King battles still with king;
Wild through the frighted air of night
    The bloody tocsins ring.

But clearer far the friendly speech
    Of scientists and seers,
The wise debate of statesmen, and
    The shouts of pioneers.

And stronger far the claspéd hands
    Of labor's teeming throngs
Who, in a hundred tongues, repeat
    Their common creeds and songs.

From shore to shore the peoples call
    In loud and sweet acclaim;
The gloom of land and sea is lit
    With pentecostal flame.

O Father, from the curse of war
    We pray thee give release;
And speed, O speed thy blesséd day
    Of justice, love, and peace.

À Hymn

Tune—"Aurelia" (Samuel Sebastian Wesley)

Note: This hymn lies in my portfolio unused, undated, and unsung. It must be classified, if at all, among my lost compositions.

To thee, O God, be homage,
　　To thee alone be praise;
Thou art our source of being,
　　The substance of our days;
Our lives thy life encircles,
　　Our paths thy law makes plain;
Beneath, above, about us
　　Thy pow'r and purpose reign.

The kings of earth are mighty,
　　But thou almighty art;
The captains claim obedience,
　　But thou command'st the heart;
The world shouts loud its mandates
　　Of sceptre and of sword;
But thy still voice declareth
　　The everlasting word.

Who doubts thee, Lord supernal?
　　Who dares thy will defy?
All thrones and empires perish
　　That thy intent deny.
We heed no other summons,
　　We hear no other call;
Thou art our God and Savior,
　　And we thy people all.

Freedom and Equality

Tune—"St. Leonard" (Henry Hiles)

Note: This hymn is unused, which is a pity, for it is perhaps the best among my hymns on the theme of brotherhood. Record and recollection seem to agree that it is a late hymn, probably written after World War II.

Thou God of all, whose spirit moves
　　From pole to silent pole;
Whose purpose binds the starry spheres
　　In one stupendous whole;
Whose life, like light, is freely poured
　　On all men 'neath the sun;
To thee we lift our hearts, and pray,
　　That thou wilt make us one.

One in the patient company
　　Of those who heed thy will,
And steadfastly pursue the way
　　Of thy commandments still;
One in the holy fellowship
　　Of those who challenge wrong,
And lift the spirit's sword to shield
　　The weak against the strong.

One in the truth that makes men free,
　　The faith that makes men brave;
One in the love that suffers long
　　To seek, and serve, and save;
One in the vision of thy peace,
　　The Kingdom yet to be—
When thou shalt be the God of all,
　　And all be one in thee.

Thy Word Alone Remaineth

Tune—"Alford" (John Bacchus Dykes)

Note: An international hymn, written in 1917 at the invitation of the Unitarian General Conference, and sung at the biennial meeting of the Conference held in Montreal, Canada, in the same year. First published in *Hymns of the Spirit* (1937).

O'er continent and ocean,
From city, field, and wood,
Still speak, O Lord, thy messengers
Of peace and brotherhood.
In Athens and Benares,
In Rome and Galilee,
They fronted kings and conquerors,
And taught mankind of thee.

We hear, O Lord, these voices,
And hail them as thine own;
They speak as speak the winds and tides
On planets far and lone:
One God, the Life of Ages;
One Rule, His Will above;
One Realm, our wide Humanity;
One Law, the Law of Love.

The tribes and nations falter
In rivalries of fear,
The fires of hate to ashes turn,
To dust, the sword and spear.
Thy word alone remaineth;
That word we speak again,
O'er sea and shore and continent,
To all the sons of men.

New Year's

Tune—"Coronation" (Oliver Holden)

Note: There is little to be said about the personal history of this hymn: not even the date is known. Published in 1937, it first appeared in *Hymns of the Spirit* of that same year.

A word may be in order about its constructive pattern of five stanzas. Of these five stanzas, the second refers to the past era of history, the third to the present, and the fourth to the future.

This arrangement is so definite and precise in the matter of line and progress of thought that it is not to be broken up. If sung at all, it is to be sung in its entirety. Yet almost never have I heard more than three or four verses used. The past, present, and future are thus cast out into oblivion.

All hail, the pageant of the years
    That endless come and go,
The brave procession of the spheres
    In Time's resistless flow—
Arise, and crown our days with good,
In glad, exultant brotherhood.

Behind us fade the centuries
    Of man at war with man,
The fierce and foul futilities
    Of battling tribe and clan—
Arise, and crown our days with good,
In glad, exultant brotherhood.

Around us lies the heritage
    Of clashing sword and shield,
The want and waste, the hate and rage
    Of many a gloried field—
Arise, and crown our days with good,
In glad, exultant brotherhood.

Behold, there looms the mystery
    Of love diviner far,
There speaks the steadfast prophecy
    Of nations freed from war—
Arise, and crown our days with good,
In glad, exultant brotherhood!

The aeons come, the aeons go,
    The stars nor pause nor cease;
On wings of silence, soft as snow,
    Shall come the boon of peace.
All hail, our days are crowned with good,
In glad, exultant brotherhood!

Trust in God

Tune—"Ewing" (Alexander Ewing)

Note: An unknown hymn, the date forgotten. Its theme is familiar, but clamors for fresh expression lest it be lost in an age that awaits a rediscovery of the deeper things of the spirit.

O God of light and darkness,
    Of evil and of good,
Thou dost not frown upon us
    In stern and angry mood;
Thou dost not send damnation
    From judgment-bar or throne,
But when in sin we falter,
    Our sorrow is thine own.

If hatred sears our spirits,
    Thy spirit bows in woe;
If fierce contention rends us,
    Thy tears in pity flow;
When war's devouring havoc
    Engulfs men in despair,
Thou into hell descendest,
    Their agony to share.

Thou wilt not lose nor leave us,
    Thy love endureth still;
Patient and calm and changeless
    Abides thy holy will.
Thine are we till the ages
    Outwatch the farthest sun,
And men at last in gladness
    Proclaim, Thy will be done!

The Voice of God Is Calling

Tune—"Webb" (George James Webb)

Note:

*Also I heard the voice of the Lord, saying, Whom shall I send,
and who will go for us? Then said I, Here am I; send me.*
ISAIAH 6:8

Written on board the S.S. *Laconia,* in September, 1913, on the
return voyage from my first trip to Europe. The hymn was sung
as the dedicatory hymn at a conference of the Young People's Religious Union in Boston, Massachusetts, in that same month. It
was first published in the *New Hymn and Tune Book* (1914).
The hymn has been widely used in this country and in England,
and has been translated into German, Spanish, and Japanese.

The voice of God is calling
    Its summons unto men;
As once he spake in Zion,
    So now he speaks again:
Whom shall I send to succor
    My people in their need?
Whom shall I send to loosen
    The bonds of shame and greed?

I hear my people crying
    In cot and mine and slum;
No field or mart is silent,
    No city street is dumb.
I see my people falling
    In darkness and despair.
Whom shall I send to shatter
    The fetters which they bear?

We heed, O Lord, thy summons,
    And answer: Here are we!
Send us upon thine errand!
    Let us thy servants be!
Our strength is dust and ashes,
    Our years a passing hour;
But thou canst use our weakness
    To magnify our power.

From ease and plenty save us,
    From pride of place absolve;
Purge us of low desire,
    Lift us to high resolve.
Take us and make us holy,
    Teach us thy will and way;
Speak, and behold we answer!
    Command, and we obey!

America Triumphant!

Tune—"Komm, Seele" (J. W. Franck)

Note: Written early in the Great War (1915) in an effort to provide a worthy patriotic hymn. This hymn has been sung, and has been introduced into newly published hymnals of our time. But I have scarcely succeeded with my purpose, nor could I expect to do so, with Katherine Lee Bates's great hymn, "O Beautiful for Spacious Skies," in my pathway.

America triumphant!
    Brave land of pioneers!
On mountain peak and prairie
    Their winding trail appears.
The wilderness is planted;
    The deserts bloom and sing;
On coast and plain the cities
    Their smoky banners fling.

America triumphant!
    New shrine of pilgrim feet!
The poor and lost and hunted
    Before thine altars meet.
From sword of czar and sultan,
    From ban of priest and peer,
To thee, o'er trackless waters,
    They come in hope and fear.

America triumphant!
    Dear homeland of the free!
Thy sons have fought and fallen
    To win release for thee.
They broke the chains of empire;
    They smote the wrongs of state;
And lies of law and custom
    They blasted with their hate.

America triumphant!
    Grasp firm thy sword and shield!
Not yet have all thy foemen
    Been driven from the field.
They lurk by forge and market,
    They hide in mine and mill;
And bold with greed of conquest
    They flout thy blesséd will.

America, America!
    Triumphant thou shalt be!
Thy hills and vales shall echo
    The shouts of liberty.
Thy bards shall sing thy glory,
    Thy prophets tell thy praise,
And all thy sons and daughters
    Acclaim thy golden days!

America Belovéd

Tune—"Materna" (Samuel Augustus Ward)

Note: Written in pity and lamentation on the entrance of the United States into the Great War in April, 1917.

America belovéd!
    Thy ships are on the tide,
Thy sons from farm and factory
    The paths of ocean ride;
On Flanders Field, baptized of blood,
    They guard the sacred sod,
And all their fair young lives lay down
    For country and for God.

America belovéd!
    Thou sendest these to die,
On altars tall and beautiful
    Such offerings should lie.
What sins soe'er despoil thy fame,
    What idle wantonings,
Confess, and in confession purge
    The land of bitter things.

Lift up the weak and fallen;
    Put down the great and proud;
Emancipate the multitudes
    With want and labor bowed;
Scourge prejudice and hate and lust;
    Guard truth and equity;
From shore to shore, from heart to heart,
    Extend democracy!

Then, O belovéd country,
    Thy sons shall not in vain
Drink, in the bitter cup of wrath,
    The dregs of death and pain.
Thou shalt be free, and freedom bring
    To nations near and far,
And end, in peace and brotherhood,
    The waste and woe of war.

For a Church Organist

Tune—"The Community Church" (Clifford Demarest)

Note:

Jubal—the father of all such as handle the harp and pipe.

GENESIS 4:21

Written for the twenty-fifth anniversary of Clifford Demarest as organist of the Community Church of New York, on May 10, 1936.

His composition (*above*) is an interesting tour de force in the case of music in praise of God.

Old Jubal twanged the bowstring,
    And heard a humming sound;
He cut wild reeds, and in them
    Sweet arias he found;
He stretched raw skins, and beat them
    In rude and rhythmic roar;
And lo, the tides of music
    His waking soul upbore.

From age to age new Jubals
    In ecstasy have wrought;
In lute and pipe and sackbut
    New melodies have sought;
Till now, in pulsing organ,
    In orchestra and choir,
They lead the ardent spirit
    To conquer and aspire.

O God, thou art the secret
    The Jubals seek and find;
In stars and suns and oceans
    Are harmonies designed.
Thou art the song and singer,
    The instrument and tone;
In thee be jubilation,
    To thee be praise, alone!

Book II

The Burning of the Church

Tune—"Coniston" (Joseph Barnby)

Note: Written on the occasion of the burning of the Church of the Messiah (the Community Church) on September 11, 1919. The hymn was sung at the union services held by All Souls (Unitarian) Church of New York on the following Sunday, September 18.

Behold, O God! our holy house
    And beautiful is burned;
The altars by our fathers reared
    To dust and ashes turned.

We stand as those who driven far
    By waste of fire and sword,
Find not in unfamiliar ways
    The presence of the Lord.

But lo, through storm and flame there fly
    Words winged of faith and love;
Quick to our sudden need are friends,
    Like angels from above.

This strange and crowded world becomes
    One vast cathedral fair;
And every humblest heart of man,
    An altar for our prayer.

We have thee, Lord. Our house is dust,
    But thou art living still
Within the loved community
    Of souls that do thy will.

Hymn of Dedication

Tune—"Lancashire" (Henry Smart)

Note: Written on the occasion of the dedication of the rebuilt Community Church on December 31, 1922.

O Father, for this temple
    Our thanks to thee we raise;
Our ashes turned to Beauty,
    Our heaviness to Praise.
The waste anew is builded,
    The desolation healed;
Our sacrifice and labor
    By thy great mercy sealed.

Accept, O Lord, this temple,
    An offering to thee;
Make it a sign prophetic
    Of days that yet shall be—
Its rock-hewn base the Justice
    That holds the stars in awe;
Its walls the Love triumphant
    That vindicates thy Law.

Here may the quest of knowledge
    Be loos'd of bar and ban;
Truth be the holy passion
    That mingles man with man.
Let Freedom like a beacon
    Upon a headland sheer,
Flame high amid the darkness
    Of bigotry and fear.

Let no man here be stranger,
    No heart by hate undone;
Jew, Gentile, Christian, pagan,
    Negro and white, be one.
One fellowship of comrades
    In love revealing thee!
So comes on earth thy kingdom,
    The world's community.

On the Dedication of a Chapel

Tune—"Winchester Old" (Christopher Tye)

Note: Written for the dedication, on Sunday, October 31, 1943, of the Chapel in the rebuilt Community Church.

Accept, O Lord, this precious gift
    Which hand and heart have wrought—
This altar where the soul may lift
    To thee its holiest thought.

Within these walls may prayers be said
    For all who seek thy rest;
All sorrow here be comforted,
    All happiness be blest.

Lo, silence, like an evening's calm,
    Breathes quiet from above;
And sweet distills the spirit's balm
    Of faith, and hope, and love.

A Hymn of Progress

Tune—"All Saints New" (Henry Stephen Cutler)

Note: Written on the occasion of the one hundredth anniversary of the founding of the Community Church of New York in March, 1925.

When darkness, brooding o'er the deep,
    Disclosed nor stars nor sun;
When steaming seas, in awful calm,
    Knew not a world begun;
Thy spirit, Lord, was in the void,
    Thy purpose moved the night,
And loud through aeons wonderful,
    Proclaimed: Let there be Light!

The sons of men the summons heard,
    And starting from the sod,
They stretched their feebly groping hands
    Out toward the ways of God;
They stood erect on trembling feet,
    With dim and fearful sight,
And moving lips unused of speech,
    Cried out: Let there be Light!

The centuries, like marching stars,
    Have flamed, and dimmed away;
Still onward strives the human host
    From darkness into day;
The saints, the prophets, and the seers,
    The martyrs calmly free,
Blaze high and far the sacred way
    To Truth and Liberty.

Our fathers, Lord, a humble band,
    Walked gallantly this path;
Sought desert ways of solitude,
    Dared storms of hate and wrath.
We follow where they bravely trod,
    Hold firm the fields they won—
Vouchsafe, O God, we fail thee not,
    Until thy work be done!

Anniversary (1)

Tune—"Ernan" (Lowell Mason)

Note: Written on the occasion of my twenty-fifth anniversary as minister of the Community Church in 1932.

Great Spirit of the speeding spheres,
Whose constant orbits mark the years,
Whose tides arise, then flow apart,
As pulse-beats of the cosmic heart,

Thou, God, to whom an aeon gone
Is but as yesterday when done,
The centuries' march of tribe and clan
The shadow of a moment's span;

How canst thou know our transient days?
Why shouldst thou trace our trivial ways?
Why hold within thine awful hand
These motes of dust, these grains of sand?

Yet we are thine! Th' eternal flood
Flows through the currents of our blood,
Th' undying fire of star and sun
Kindles our souls, and makes them one.

One with thy life, ere time began,
Nor knew the rise and fall of man;
One till the numbered years are fled,
And earth to cold and darkness sped!

Teach us, O God, the purpose high
Which moves the spaces of the sky,
That our quick day, from error free,
May live in thine eternity.

Anniversary (2)

Tune—"Ellacombe" (Anon.)

Note: Written in 1947, on the occasion of my fortieth anniversary as the minister of the Community Church.

Bright visions glow across the sky
    Of brotherhood and peace;
Brave voices summon from on high
    To bring mankind release;
But still in bonds of hate and fear
    The world in anguish lies,
And lists from year to weary year
    Men's bitter moans and cries.

The seers have seen and shown the way,
    And brave that way have trod;
The prophets have proclaimed the day
    Revealed to them of God;
The saints have lived, the martyrs died,
    To bring the Kingdom in;
But lo, in triumph still abide
    The tyrannies of sin.

How long, O Lord, must thy great law
    Still be on earth undone?
When shall we hold thy will in awe,
    And make our wills thine own?
The visions glow, the voices call;
    This is thy promised day;
We pledge thee, Lord, whate'er befall,
    To follow in thy way.

Anniversary (3)

Tune—"St. Matthew" (William Croft)

Note: Written in 1949 to celebrate my retirement from the active
ministry on November 29 of the same year.

To earth's remote horizons,
　　Far-flung from pole to pole,
Where planets burn and beckon,
　　And distant oceans roll.
There run the age-old tidings,
　　A prophecy sublime,
Of God's eternal Kingdom
　　In every coast and clime.

It comes, this promised Kingdom,
　　To give mankind release
From fear and hate and discord
　　To love and joy and peace.
No sword can stay its progress,
　　No sceptre break its power;
The stars make proclamation
　　Of God's appointed hour.

High o'er the flags of nations
　　Looms Christ's eternal cross,
It waits, and watches empires
　　Become as dust and dross;
It reaches arms of pity
　　To clan at war with clan;
It blazons forth God's purpose—
　　The brotherhood of man.

Arise, ye stricken peoples,
　　Unite with hand and heart
To smite the bounds and barriers
　　That hold mankind apart;
The Kingdom, O the Kingdom,
　　The reign of God begun!
His law at last triumphant
　　His will in fullness done.

Arise, Ye Peoples

Tune—"Missionary Hymn" (Lowell Mason)

Note: This hymn may fittingly be called Mr. Donald G. Harrington's hymn. It was written for his installation as associate minister of the Community Church, in anticipation of his assumption of full office in 1949.

Thy voice, O God, in every age
    By prophet souls is heard.
No time or place has been denied
    The guidance of thy word.
It spake in thunder from the slope
    Of Sinai's flaming core;
And echoed o'er the quiet waves
    By Jordan's lonely shore.

To us, O Lord, this latter day,
    Proclaim thy holy will;
Point us the straight and narrow path
    Our feet must follow still.
And to this youth of prophet-line
    Send stern and high command,
That in the service of thy cause
    He may do all, and stand.

Touch thou his lips, in this his morn,
    With coals of living fire;
Lift thou his heart, on wings of power,
    To heights of pure desire.
Grant him a vision far beyond
    The present pain and plight,
That he may upward lead mankind
    From darkness into light.

Ordination

Tune—"Marton" (Marton Iszlai)

Note: The election and ordination of Dana McLean Greeley as President of the American Unitarian Association, in succession to Frederick May Eliot, was an event of large importance in the history of Unitarianism.

For the Ordination Service, held at the Arlington Street Church in Boston on October 7, 1958, this hymn was written.

Bless thou, O God, this fellowship
    Of brave and stalwart souls,
Who seek on earth to do thy will,
    To meet thy farthest goals;
No cowardice to weaken us,
    No compromise betray,
But all, in faithful fortitude,
    Thy purpose to obey.

And him, our servant, tried of God,
    Who hears and heeds thy call,
Give strength to climb the tow'ring steep
    Nor faint, nor fail, nor fall;
Touch thou his lips with sacred fire,
    Snatched from thine altars tall,
Trust him to speak the needful word,
    Thy kingdom to install.

To thee alone, O God, we bow,
    In thee are lifted up,
With thee we seek the Holy Grail,
    Love's lost communion cup;
Until at last, at one with thee,
    In love's divine accord,
We find, in righteousness and peace,
    The wisdom of the Lord.

The Isles of Shoals (1)

Tune—"Evangel" (Gottfried Wilhelm Fine)

Note: Written in 1907 at the Isles of Shoals, off Portsmouth, New Hampshire, for the *Isles of Shoals Hymn Book* (1908). This hymn was included in the *New Hymn and Tune Book* (1914) with revisions sanctioned by the author.

O God, whose smile is in the sky,
    Whose path is in the sea,
Once more from earth's tumultuous strife
    We gladly turn to thee.
Once more to thee our songs we sing,
    Once more our prayers we raise,
And for the refuge of these isles
    Give thee our deepest praise.

Here all the myriad sounds of earth
    In solemn stillness die,
While wind and wave unite to chant
    Their anthems to the sky;
Far, far away the heat and dust
    And panting of the race, .
While here, in Nature's temple vast,
    We meet thee face to face.

We come as those with toil far spent
    Who crave for rest and peace,
And from the care and fret of life
    Would find in thee release;
We come as those who yearn to know
    The truth that makes men free;
And feel the love that binds us each
    To all, and all to thee.

O Father, soothe all troubled thought,
    Dispel all idle fear,
Purge every heart of secret sin,
    And banish every care;
Until, as shine upon the seas
    The silent stars above,
There shines upon our trusting souls
    The light of thine own love.

The Isles of Shoals (2)

Tune—"Meirionydd" (William Lloyd)

Also set to the following original tune by Robert Buxton, organist and teacher:

Note: Written at the Isles of Shoals in the summer of 1930. The tune above was composed later in the same year.

O blesséd isle of quiet,
    Rock-rooted in the sea,
Thy firm foundations plumb the gulf
    Of earth's immensity.
What though the ocean rages,
    What though the blast alarms?
Deep under deep, there rest secure
    The everlasting arms!

O blesséd isle of vision,
    Engirdled by the sea,
Out to the farthest span of space
    Thy vista reaches free;
To east the glow of dawning,
    To west the blaze of night,
Round all the long horizon's rim
    The everlasting light!

O blesséd isle of friendship
    Enshrined upon the sea,
To kneel within thy stony fane
    The world we gladly flee;
And in the mystic silence,
    Slow-wafted from above,
Find hand in hand, and heart with heart,
    The everlasting love!

Two Hymns to One Tune

Tune—"Potsdam" (Johann Sebastian Bach)

I

A Hymn for the Church

Note: The first hymn was written for the Community Church of New York; the second hymn for the Shore Road Academy in Brooklyn, New York. The former was first published in the *Christian Century* in 1936, and was included in *Hymns of the Spirit* (1937).

Show us thy way, O God!
    Our feet have wandered far.
We seek the path thy saints have trod,
    Where peace and beauty are.

Teach us thy word, O God!
    Subdue earth's racking din;
That we may hear at home, abroad,
    The still, small voice within.

Tell us thy will, O God!
    Our own we cannot trust.
We seek the summons of thy rod
    To raise us from the dust.

Thy way, thy word, thy will—
    These are our surest guides
To bring us where thy spirit still
    In holiness abides.

II
A Hymn for the School

God of the searching mind,
    Help us thy truth to find,
That we may gaze, from error free,
    With single eye on thee.

God of the loving heart,
    Teach us our humble part—
To live in kindness unto all
    Thy creatures great and small.

God of th' aspiring soul,
    Point onward to thy goal,
That we, with eager strength and grace,
    May run the spirit's race.

Our teacher and our friend,
    More of thy wisdom lend,
That we in virtue may increase,
    And find at last thy peace.

A Christmas Hymn

Tune—"Carol" (Richard Storrs Willis)

Note: Christmas hymns, anthems, and carols are trite. Year after year they say the same thing in the same way. Seldom does there emerge out of the mass a Brooks's "O Little Town of Bethlehem" or a Sears's "It Came Upon a Midnight Clear" to catch a touch of inspiration and sing its way into every heart.

This hymn is an attempt to tell the Christmas story anew, with a new scenario, a new setting in time and place, a new motif. It is a Christmas hymn for our day, and must succeed or fail in this pattern and purpose.

The Bethlehem stars are dim tonight,
 The Bethlehem skies are still,
The weary shepherds sleep among
 Their flocks upon the hill;
But Caesar's legions guard the gate,
 His trumpets wait the morn;
Why come not angels to proclaim
 The Son of Man is born?

The Bethlehem streets are dark tonight,
 The Bethlehem winds are cold;
A hungry jackal howls his pain
 Out on the empty wold:
But Caesar's banners flaunt their wings
 Athwart the torches' glare
On soldiers in a stable-yard—
 Why comes not Mary there?

O Bethlehem town, our hearts tonight
 Are dreaming all of thee;
Hast thou no song for us to hear,
 No star for us to see?
Must Caesar's trumpets cry the doom
 Of God's dread Judgment Day,
Or shall we find thy peace again,
 And at a manger pray?

Book III

America

Tune—"America" (Harmonia Anglicana)

Note: Written in 1939, this hymn has a few good lines, but on the whole is commonplace. Still, it sings well, which is undoubtedly due to the fact that the hymn is frankly in imitation of "America."

God save the people's cause,
Justice and equal laws,
    Freedom and right.
Save us from tyranny,
Fear, hate, and slavery,
From war's iniquity,
    In this black night.

God of the peoples all,
Hear thou our desp'rate call
    From shore to shore.
Sustain the true and brave,
The weak and helpless save,
Bring in the peace we crave,
    For evermore.

O thou who reign'st above,
Lord of all Truth and Love,
    Our spirits' Home,
Forgive the sin we bear,
Purge us of dark despair,
Confirm the faith we dare—
    Thy Kingdom come!

Onward, Upward

Tune—"St. Gertrude" (Sir Arthur Sullivan)

Note: Dedicated to the American Unitarian Association on the occasion of the one hundred and twenty-fifth anniversary of its founding (1825-1950).

Onward still and upward,
    With our courage high,
Follow we the vision
    Glowing in the sky;
Dark the way before us,
    Steep the path and long,
Climb we still undaunted,
    Chanting loud our song:

        CHORUS: *Onward still and upward,*
                With our courage high,
            Follow we the vision,
                Glowing in the sky.

What though storms engulf us,
    What though foes assail;
'Gainst our stern endeavor,
    These shall not prevail;
Hands and hearts united,
    In one purpose strong;
Lift we now our voices
    In resounding song:

        CHORUS: *Onward still,* ETC.

God who fails us never
    Leads the way we go;
Points us to the Kingdom,
    Promised here below;
To his name forever,
    Prayer and praise belong,
His our one allegiance,
    His our triumph song:

        CHORUS: *Onward still,* ETC.

A Hymn of Wrath Against Child Labor

Tune—"Brattle Street" (Ignaz Joseph Pleyel)

Note: This hymn and the following hymn, "For the Bondmen of Labor," were the first hymns I ever wrote. I do not remember their precise order. Both belong to the period before the Great War (1914-1918).

I find significance in the fact that my first attempts at hymn-writing took the form of social hymns, which were scarce at that age, but which we see abundantly in ours. Gladden, Higginson, North, and Anna Garlin Spencer are some of the writers who led the way in this renaissance of social thinking and feeling.

O God, whose justice is a rod
    That smites our human greed,
Whose mercy is a healing balm
    For hearts that break and bleed—
We cry to thee, O Lord, for strength
    To right the wrongs of earth,
To lift the yokes and burst the bonds
    That make a curse of birth.

We pray thee for these little ones
    Who toil in mine and mill,
Whose moans of pain and weariness
    No clanking wheels can still;
Whose backs are bent, whose eyes are dim,
    Whose feet are halt and lamed,
With little hands all gnarled and torn,
    And bodies bruised and maimed.

O Father, are these children thine,
    Who never play nor sing,
Who ne'er with shouts of boist'rous glee
    Make woods and pastures ring;
Who know all manhood's stress and strain
    Ere manhood's strength is won,
Who taste the bitterness of life
    Ere life is scarce begun?

Lay bare, O God, thy mighty arm,
    Ungird thy sword of death;
The lust that feeds on children's blood
    Smite with thine awful wrath.
So, in thy mercy, from their bonds
    These little ones release,
And give them air and sun and play,
    And joy and love and peace.

For the Bondmen of Labor

Tune—"Brattle Street" (Ignaz Joseph Pleyel)

Note: See the preceding hymn, "A Hymn of Wrath Against Child Labor."

Almighty God, beneath whose eye
    No sparrow falls in vain,
Who giveth free to high and low
    The sunshine and the rain;
Amid the darkness of our days
    We turn to thee for light,
And to thy will we make appeal
    For justice and for right.

Behold, O God, the myriad throngs
    Who toil from sun to sun,
The bondmen of the forge and shaft
    Whose tasks are never done;
Behold them pile, in sweat and tears,
    The wealth of kingly lands,
And in their hours of patient prayer
    To thee lift empty hands.

The wandering sunbeams meet them not,
    The breezes pass them by,
Fettered in mine and mill and slum,
    They helpless live and die.
For them no poet dreams his dream,
    No prophet speaks his word,
The raptured song of saint and seer
    Trembles and thrills unheard.

Almighty God, behold thy will
    Flouted and scorned and shamed;
Behold these children of thy heart
    Burdened and robbed and maimed;
Lift high thy sword of love, and smite
    The greed of power and place,
And to the least of these restore
    The bounties of thy grace.

A Providence of Love

Tune—"Hamburg" (Lowell Mason)

Note: This hymn was written for the *Beacon Song and Service Book* (1908), included in the *New Hymn and Tune Book* (1914) and in *Hymns of the Spirit* (1937). It is a starkly simple piece, which has found wide acceptance among the churches.

O Father, thou who givest all
The bounty of thy perfect love,
We thank thee that upon us fall
Such tender blessings from above.

We thank thee for the grace of home,
For mother's love and father's care;
For friends and teachers—all who come
Our joys and hopes and fears to share.

For eyes to see and ears to hear,
For hands to serve and arms to lift,
For shoulders broad and strong to bear,
For feet to run on errands swift.

For faith to conquer doubt and fear,
For love to answer every call,
For strength to do, and will to dare,
We thank thee, O thou Lord of all!

God in All

Tune—"Beatitudo" (John Bacchus Dykes)

Note: This hymn is one of my earlier hymns, the exact date of which has been lost.

In 1957 there appeared a new Anglican hymnal entitled *Hymns of the Faith*. It was published by the Oxford University Press for use in Worcester Cathedral. Hymn No. 602 is this hymn, "O God, Whose Love is Over All," sadly mutilated, but its integrity not quite spoiled. It is interesting to see this hymn attributed to "J. H. Holmes."

O God, whose love is over all
    The children of thy grace,
Whose rich and tender blessings fall
    On every age and place;
Hear thou the songs and prayers we raise
    In eager joy to thee,
And teach us, as we sound thy praise,
    In all things thee to see.

To see thee in the sun by day,
    And in the stars by night,
In waving grass and ocean spray,
    And leaves and flowers bright;
To hear thy voice, like spoken word,
    In every breeze that blows,
In every song of every bird,
    And every brook that flows.

To see thee in each quiet home,
    Where faith and love abide,
In school and church, where all may come,
    To seek thee side by side;
To see thee in each human life,
    Each struggling human heart,
Each path by which, in eager strife,
    Men seek the better part.

Bells and Songs

A Christmas Carol for Children (1)

Tune—"St. Louis" (Lewis Henry Redner)

Note: I have included in this book two Christmas carols for children, both of which are unsatisfactory, the most unsatisfactory pieces in the collection. But they make plain my purpose, which is to illustrate the new type of Christmas hymnology that even now is on the way.

O hear the ringing of the bells,
  The bells of Christmas morn!
O heed the tale their music tells,
  The tale of Christmas morn!
Of wisemen journeying through the night,
  Of shepherds glist'ring bright,
Of angels singing their delight—
  The tale that Christ is born!

O hear the songs the children sing,
  The songs of Christmas Day!
O heed the joy their voices bring,
  The joy of Christmas Day!
Of homes a-gleam with faces dear,
  Of hearts aglow with cheer,
Of love that casteth out all fear—
  The joy of Christ for aye!

Where?

A Christmas Carol for Children (2)

Tune—"Duke Street" (John Hatton)

Note: See the immediately preceding hymn, "Bells and Songs: A Christmas Carol for Children (1)." See also "A Christmas Hymn" on page 73.

Where ring the Christmas bells tonight?
    In homes aglow with festal light,
    In hearts with love and laughter bright,
There ring the Christmas bells tonight.

Where sing the angel hosts today?
    Where men the will of Christ obey,
    And for his Kingdom work and pray,
There sing the angel hosts today.

A Jewish Hymn

Tune—"Yigdal" (Jewish melody, arr. by Meyer Lyon)

Note: Dedicated to Rabbi Stephen S. Wise and the Free Synagogue
in New York City, and sung on April 17, 1932, at the twenty-fifth
anniversary of the founding of the Synagogue.

The flames of Sinai clothe no more
    The presence of the Lord;
The desert winds no echoes bear
    Of Moses' thund'rous word;
Yet still in wildernesses far
    Moves Israel's chosen band,
Resolv'd through want and waste and woe
    To find the Promised Land.

Dust unto dust, Hosea's bones
    Lie deep in Zion's sod;
The ashes of the centuries hide
    The stones Isaiah trod;
Yet still on Israel's altars burn
    The fires of prophecy,
And lips with living coals are touched
    The doom of sin to cry.

O God of Israel, not in vain
    Thy sons proclaimed thy law;
The witness born on Judah's hills
    Holds still a world in awe;
And lo, today in this far land,
    In him, thy servant true,
In these thy people, strong and free,
    Thy spirit lives anew.

In Memoriam: Leo Tolstoi

Tune—"O Jesu" (John Balthazar Reimann)

Note: This hymn was written in reverent memory of a great man, and was sung at the religious service held in his honor on the centennial of his birth (1928).

I know of but one other hymn of the kind—namely, Jan Struthers' profoundly moving "When Stephen, Full of Power and Grace," a tribute to the first Christian martyr.

Biographical preaching is among the most effective of homiletical forms. The worship of great men is religion in its best estate. Thomas Carlyle said: "All things that we see standing accomplished in the world are properly the outer material result, the practical realization and embodiment, of Thoughts that dwelt in the Great Men sent into the world."

The Tolstoi hymn, as published here, may be taken as an example of what can be done. In this hope, may other hymnists "go and do likewise."

A spirit walks the heedless earth,
    Majestic, stern, benign;
A presence lights the ways of men
    With radiance divine:
Arise, ye peoples, follow on;
God's Kingdom here can still be won.

He looks on kings and conquerors—
    And lo, their swords are dust;
He fronts the rich—and all their goods
    Are given to moth and rust:
Arise, ye peoples, follow on;
God's Kingdom here can still be won.

He speaks—and thrones and altars shake
    Beneath his thund'rous word;
He calls—and myriads hear again
    The calling of the Lord:
Arise, ye peoples, follow on;
God's Kingdom here can still be won.

His smock reveals the seamless robe
    Wherein the Master trod;
The furrow of his plow becomes
    The highway of our God:
Arise, ye peoples, follow on;
God's Kingdom here can still be won.

With saints and seers of all the years
    He points the holy way;
The stout of heart, with courage high,
    Will walk with him today:
Arise, ye peoples, follow on;
God's Kingdom here shall yet be won!

God's Providence

Tune—"Forest Green" (Anon.)

Note: A vesper hymn, written early and undated. It is an instance of a deliberate attempt to write an evening hymn, and lacks only the material and reason for composition. Compare this hymn with the following hymn, "Sweet and Low," and note the difference.

Almighty God, to whom the dark
    Is even as the light,
We thank thee that thou flee'st not
    As day fades into night;
But, when the stars like beacons flame
    In heaven's unmeasured deep,
Thou with the shadows drawest near,
    To guard us while we sleep.

We thank thee, Father, when we wake,
    That we are still with thee,
And guided by thy loving hand
    Wherever we may be.
In work or play, in joy or grief,
    In triumph or defeat,
Thou still art near to lead aright
    Our weak and stumbling feet.

We thank thee, Father, that each hour
    Of night and day is thine,
That both the darkness and the light
    Are by thy grace divine.
O Father, grant that more and more
    Thy presence we may see,
And every hour may dedicate
    An offering, unto thee.

Sweet and Low

Tune—"St. Anne" (William Croft)

Note: Finis and Benediction.

Be with us, Father, in this place,
    Whence care and trouble flee,
That we may know, by thy dear grace,
    How safe we are with thee.

Reach us thy hand, that we may feel,
    Thy presence with us still,
And thy sweet spirit softly steal
    Our empty hearts to fill.

Our burdens lift, our sorrows lave
    With comfort's healing balm;
Our anxious souls possess and save
    To confidence and calm.

What though the world asunder break,
    We will not faint, nor fear;
Our steadfastness no storm can shake
    If thou be ever near.

In the cool chambers of the mind,
    Silent, serene, secure,
We wait thy coming, Lord, and find
    The peace that shall endure.

Index of First Lines